ENTP: MY BRAIN HAS TOO MANY TABS OPEN

Excuse Me While I Change the World

Asa Eccleston-Kibilski

CONTENTS

WELCOME TO THE THOUGHT TORNADO

If your brain feels like a swirling vortex of ideas, half-formed plans, random trivia, and the beginning of about a dozen different arguments, congratulations! You might be an ENTP. We're the ones who see patterns others miss, question everything with relentless enthusiasm, and bore easily if life gets too predictable.

Introducing the ENTP

The ENTP personality type (also known as "the Debater" or "the Visionary") is defined by a few key traits:

- **Extroverted Intuition:** Our superpower is spotting possibilities, making connections, and brainstorming on a ridiculous scale. We live in a world of "what if?"
- **Introverted Thinking:** We analyze everything, seeking logical consistency (even if our arguments take wild turns others can't follow).
- **Extroverted Feeling:** Though sometimes emotionally awkward, we crave genuine connection and are surprisingly sensitive beneath our bravado.
- **Introverted Sensing:** Details, routines, and traditions? Not our strong suit. We're big-picture thinkers who sometimes trip over the mundane.

Life on the Inside

Imagine your mind as a browser with way too many tabs open. There's a fascinating article on quantum physics, a debate about whether hotdogs are sandwiches, a half-baked business plan, the lyrics to a song you can't get out of your head, and a philosophical quandary about the nature of existence. All equally important, all demanding attention. That's ENTP life in a nutshell.

Sound exhausting? It can be. But the flip side is a constant thrill of discovery. The world is our playground, and boredom is our worst enemy. We're drawn to novelty, complexity, and intellectual challenge like moths to a flame.

The Benefits...and the Challenges

ENTPs are the innovators, the disruptors, the ones who can't stand to leave a good idea unexplored. We see the flaws in systems, the potential in underdogs, and the humor in life's absurdities. That said, we also have a tendency to:

- Procrastinate like it's an art form
- Overanalyze simple decisions
- Start arguments for the sheer fun of it
- Get sidetracked...a lot
- Forget about practical matters like eating and paying bills

If This Sounds Familiar...

This book is for you. Whether you're a confirmed ENTP, suspect you might be, or simply love someone whose brain operates at warp speed, you're in for a wild ride. We'll delve into the ENTP experience with humor, honesty, and strategies for not just surviving, but thriving, with our whirlwind minds.

Buckle up, because the thought tornado is about to take off!

IDEA OVERLOAD: WHEN INSPIRATION BECOMES A CURSE

Picture this: you wake up with a brilliant idea. It's revolutionary, game-changing, and completely irresistible. You start outlining, researching, and sketching out plans, feeling the thrill of possibility. A few hours later, another idea strikes – equally amazing, and just as demanding of your attention. Now you're juggling two projects...and then another hits you. And another.

Welcome to the wonderful and maddening world of the ENTP idea machine.

The Blessing (and Curse) of Extroverted Intuition

Our dominant function, Extroverted Intuition (Ne), is a relentless generator of possibilities. We see patterns and connections everywhere, and the potential in just about anything. It's like having a spotlight that constantly roams the world, picking out intriguing new things to illuminate.

The upside? ENTPs are fountains of creativity, problem-solvers who think outside the box, and endlessly entertaining conversationalists. We're the ones who brainstorm solutions others haven't considered and spot opportunities hiding in plain sight.

The downside? Our brains can feel like a popcorn machine on overdrive. It's exciting, but also overwhelming – especially when combined with our tendency to see potential in EVERYTHING. That means...

- **Too many choices:** We can freeze up due to the sheer number of awesome things we could be doing.
- **Shiny object syndrome:** A new idea can easily derail an old one, making it difficult to follow through.

- **Scattered energy**: Hopping between projects makes it hard to gain deep focus or see things to completion.
- **Burnout:** When there are always more ideas to chase, it's easy to overextend ourselves.

Taming the Beast: Strategies for Idea Management

1. **The Brain Dump:** When your head's buzzing, get it ALL out. Write every idea, plan, or inspiration down, no matter how silly or incomplete.
2. **Prioritize ruthlessly:** Is this idea exciting? Does it align with your goals? Is it actually feasible? Be honest, and give a potential project the "good, better, best" treatment
3. **"Parking Lot":** Create a dedicated space for the ideas you love but can't take on right now. Revisit them periodically.
4. **Focus on one thing (for now):** It might feel restrictive, but picking a single project gives you the chance to gain momentum and actually *finish* something.
5. **Embrace mini-projects:** Need variety? Set aside time for quick brainstorming sessions, creative experiments, or exploring a new topic just for fun.

It's Not About Killing the Inspiration

The goal isn't to become a dull, predictable drone. It's about channeling our ENTP brilliance effectively. We need systems to sort and prioritize our ideas, alongside the freedom to explore.

Remember, a mind like ours is a gift. With a bit of management, all those amazing ideas can lead to amazing things.

THE DEVIL'S ADVOCATE WITHIN: WHY WE CAN'T HELP BUT DEBATE

If you've ever had an ENTP in your life, you've probably experienced The Debate. It might start innocently – a casual comment, a news headline, a seemingly obvious fact. But before you know it, you're knee-deep in an intense argument where the ENTP is gleefully challenging every assumption you have. What's going on here?

Understanding the ENTP's Love of Debate

1. **Intellectual play:** For ENTPs, debate is like a mental sport. It's a way to flex our thinking muscles, explore new perspectives, and test the limits of an idea.
2. **Truth seekers:** We're driven by a desire to find the most logical, well-reasoned position. It's not about *winning* as much as it is about getting closer to the truth.
3. **Spotting inconsistencies:** ENTPs have a knack for noticing flaws in arguments, holes in logic, or unexamined assumptions. It's almost irresistible to point them out.
4. **Mental agility:** We enjoy the challenge of arguing from different viewpoints, even ones we don't necessarily agree with. It's like a mental puzzle that sharpens our thinking.
5. **A touch of mischief:** Let's be honest, sometimes we poke the bear just for the fun of seeing what happens.

The Dark Side of Debate

Our tendency to take opposing viewpoints can be misinterpreted as:

- **Contrarianism:** Being argumentative for the sake of it, regardless of the topic.

- **Insensitivity:** Failing to recognize when a debate is causing someone else emotional distress.
- **Intellectual arrogance:** Acting like we're always the smartest person in the room.
- **Disinterest:** When we seem to be more focused on the argument than the actual issue at hand.

How to Survive (and Thrive) in an ENTP Debate

- **Don't take it personally:** 95% of the time, it's about the idea, not you.
- **Assume positive intent:** ENTPs usually want to *understand*, not just tear your argument down.
- **Stay curious:** Ask questions like "Help me see your side" or "Why is this important to you?"
- **Set boundaries:** If you're not in the mood, it's okay to say "Let's table this for another time."
- **Find common ground:** Remind the ENTP of what you DO agree on to bring the debate back to a productive space.

For the ENTPs: Tips for Debating Productively

- **Choose your battles:** Is this debate *worth* having? Are people open to hearing your perspective?
- **Read the room:** Is this playful banter or is someone actually getting upset? ENTP sarcasm doesn't always translate.
- **Focus on listening:** A good debate is a two-way street. Let others finish their thoughts.
- **Acknowledge good points:** Show that you're not just out to "win", but are genuinely evaluating ideas.
- **It's okay to agree to disagree:** Not every debate needs a resolution.

The Gift of Debate

When channeled well, our debating tendencies can lead to amazing things. We can expose flawed thinking, push for innovation, and help others see things from fresh perspectives. At our best, ENTPs are like intellectual catalysts, sparking deeper understanding and progress.

THE ASSERTIVE ENTP: A FORCE OF NATURE AND BRILLIANCE

Ah, the Assertive ENTP – a captivating blend of intellectual firecracker, charismatic leader, and relentless innovator. You, my friend, are a force of nature, a whirlwind of ideas, and a captivating presence that can light up any room. Unlike your Turbulent counterparts, you navigate the world with an unshakeable confidence and an unwavering belief in your ability to shape reality according to your vision.

Understanding the "A" in Assertive

The "A" in your Myers-Briggs code signifies that you are more outwardly focused and decisive. You tend to process information quickly and confidently, trusting your instincts and readily expressing your thoughts and opinions. This assertiveness is not about aggression, but rather a clear and direct communication style, coupled with a strong sense of self-assuredness.

The Strengths of the Assertive ENTP

- **Natural Leader:** You possess an innate ability to inspire and motivate others. Your enthusiasm is contagious, your vision is clear, and your confidence draws people in. You thrive in leadership roles, easily navigating challenges and rallying your team towards ambitious goals.
- **Master of Debate:** Intellectual sparring is your playground. You relish the opportunity to dissect ideas, challenge assumptions, and arrive at the most logical conclusion. Your wit is sharp, your arguments are well-constructed, and you have a knack for dismantling flawed logic with grace and humor.
- **Action Hero:** While some get lost in the labyrinth of ideas, you crave action. You don't just theorize, you

materialize your brilliant concepts into tangible results. Your decisiveness and go-getter attitude make you a powerful force for change in any environment.

The Challenges of the Assertive ENTP

Even the most brilliant personalities have blind spots. Here are some potential pitfalls to navigate:

- **Tunnel Vision:** Your laser focus on your own vision can sometimes lead you to disregard alternative perspectives. Make a conscious effort to listen to opposing viewpoints, even if you ultimately disagree. You might be surprised by the valuable insights you glean.

- **Blunt Honesty:** Your direct communication style, while refreshing, can sometimes come across as harsh or insensitive. Learn to deliver your critiques with tact and consider the emotional impact of your words. Remember, even the most brilliant truth bomb leaves little room for collaboration if it explodes in someone's face.

- **Restlessness:** Your constant need for novelty and stimulation can lead to boredom and a tendency to jump ship from project to project before seeing them through to completion. Embrace the power of focus and cultivate the discipline to see your endeavors through to fruition.

Maximizing Your Assertive Potential

To truly harness your remarkable potential, consider these strategies:

- **Build Your Dream Team:** Surround yourself with individuals who complement your skillset. Seek out detail-oriented thinkers who can translate your vision into actionable plans and empathetic communicators who can bridge any communication gaps.

- **Embrace Strategic Empathy:** While your natural inclination may be toward directness, understanding the motivations and needs of others is crucial for effective leadership.

Cultivate your emotional intelligence to build stronger relationships and foster a collaborative environment.

- **Channel Your Drive:** Your boundless energy is a gift, but it can also lead to burnout. Learn to delegate tasks effectively, schedule downtime for rest and rejuvenation, and find healthy outlets for your relentless curiosity.

The Assertive ENTP Legacy

The world needs your disruptive spirit, your unwavering optimism, and your relentless pursuit of progress. Don't be afraid to challenge the status quo, champion innovative ideas, and inspire others to reach their full potential. Remember, Assertive ENTP, you are a force to be reckoned with. Use your power wisely, build a legacy of positive change, and leave a mark on the world as brilliant, bold, and undeniably you.

THE TURBULENT ENTP: A SYMPHONY OF DOUBT AND BRILLIANCE

Turbulent ENTPs, a paradox wrapped in an enigma, you are the brilliant minds who wrestle with self-doubt, the social butterflies who crave connection yet fear rejection. Your inner world is a whirlwind of ideas, possibilities, and anxieties all vying for attention. But within this seeming chaos lies a potent force for innovation and positive change, once you learn to navigate the currents of your unique personality.

Understanding the "T" in Turbulent

The "T" in your Myers-Briggs code signifies that you are more susceptible to stress and emotional reactivity than your Assertive counterparts. This doesn't make you weak, but rather highlights a different way of experiencing the world. You process information deeply, analyzing not just the logical aspects but also the emotional undercurrents. This sensitivity gives you a nuanced understanding of human behavior, but it can also leave you feeling overwhelmed by the sheer volume of stimuli.

The Struggles of the Turbulent ENTP

- **The Crippling Critic Within:** Your sharp intellect is a double-edged sword. It fuels your creativity but can also turn inwards, becoming a relentless inner critic. You may find yourself questioning your ideas, agonizing over potential failure, and holding yourself to impossibly high standards.
- **The Fear of Rejection:** While you crave social interaction and intellectual sparring, the fear of rejection can be a paralyzing force. You may overthink conversations, shy away from sharing your ideas, or struggle to connect with others on a

deeper level.

- **The Shiny Object Syndrome:** Your insatiable curiosity and love of novelty can lead to a constant chase for the next big thing. You may struggle to follow through on projects, flitting from one idea to the next without fully realizing your potential.

Harnessing Your Turbulent Power

The very traits that create challenges can also be your greatest strengths. Here's how to turn the tide:

- **Challenge Your Inner Critic:** Recognize the self-doubt for what it is – a faulty thought pattern. Practice self-compassion, celebrate your successes (no matter how small), and remind yourself that even the most brilliant minds experience moments of uncertainty.
- **Embrace Vulnerability:** It takes courage to be vulnerable and share your authentic self with others. However, building genuine connections requires openness. Don't be afraid to express your anxieties and fears – you'll be surprised by the empathy and support you find.
- **Channel Your Energy:** Combat the flitting focus by setting achievable goals, breaking down projects into manageable steps, and finding an accountability partner who can keep you on track. Remember, consistent progress, even in small doses, trumps a million half-finished ideas.

The Turbulent ENTP Advantage

Your deep empathy makes you an incredible friend and confidant. You have a unique ability to see the world from multiple perspectives, fostering understanding and building bridges across divides. When you channel your emotional intelligence, you become a powerful advocate for change, a champion for the underdog, and a voice for those who crave a more just world.

Building Your Support System

Don't underestimate the power of surrounding yourself with the right people. Seek out those who appreciate your intellectual fire but can also offer a calming presence and a listening ear. Find mentors who can guide you through periods of doubt and collaborators who share your passion for innovation.

Remember, Turbulent ENTP, you are a symphony of brilliant ideas and powerful emotions. Learn to master the instruments within you, and the world will be your stage. Embrace the beauty of your complexity, harness your strengths, and let your unique voice resonate through the world.

SOCIAL BUTTERFLIES...WITH A STING: NAVIGATING FRIENDSHIPS AS AN ENTP

ENTPs are social creatures. We thrive on engaging conversations, crave intellectual stimulation, and generally enjoy being around interesting people. Yet, our friendships can be a bit of a paradox. We're the life of the party who secretly dreads small talk, the fiercely loyal friends who sometimes disappear from the face of the earth, and the opinionated debaters who crave deep emotional connection.

The ENTP Friendship Experience: Joys and Challenges

What makes us tick in a friendship?

- **Witty banter:** We love conversations that are playful, insightful, and full of rapid-fire ideas.
- **Shared passions:** We bond deeply over common interests, especially if they're a bit offbeat or niche.
- **Intellectual sparring:** A friend who can challenge our ideas and keep up with our mental energy is pure gold.
- **Directness & Honesty:** We cut through the BS and appreciate friends who do the same.
- **Independence:** We need space to breathe and explore our own ideas without feeling clingy or constrained.

Where things can get tricky:

- **Small talk purgatory:** Superficial conversations about the weather or celebrity gossip make us want to gnaw our own arm off.
- **Overstimulation:** Too much socializing can be draining, especially if it's with people who don't 'get' our brand of humor or conversational style.

- **The vanishing act:** ENTPs can get absorbed in projects or ideas, forgetting to check in with friends for way too long.
- **Unintentional insensitivity:** Our blunt style and focus on logic can hurt feelings unintentionally, especially with more emotionally sensitive types.
- **Finding our tribe:** Not everyone appreciates our chaotic energy or love of debate, making deep connections harder to find.

Strategies for Amazing ENTP Friendships

For the ENTPs:

- **Quality over quantity:** Cultivate a few close friendships with people who appreciate your unique brand of crazy, rather than trying to be everyone's buddy.
- **Communicate your needs:** It's okay to say "I need some alone time to recharge" or "I love deep conversations, but small talk makes me itchy."
- **Practice empathy:** Pause before delivering a harsh truth and consider how it might land on your friend.
- **The check-in text:** Even a quick "Thinking of you!" text goes a long way in showing friends they matter, even when you're in a mental cave.
- **Find your people:** Seek out communities (online or IRL) where your quirky interests, humor, and love of intellectual debate are celebrated.

For friends of ENTPs:

- **Embrace the weirdness:** The best gift you can give an ENTP is to accept and enjoy their oddities.
- **Bring the interesting stuff:** Don't bore them with small talk. Share a weird news article, ask a thought-provoking question, or discuss a fascinating theory.
- **Call us on our BS (nicely):** We respect friends who can say, "Hey, that comment was kinda hurtful."
- **Initiate sometimes:** Don't take it personally if we disappear,

but a friendly nudge now and then reminds us you're there.

- **Don't expect us to be something we're not:** We won't become social butterflies who love brunch gossip. And that's okay.

The Potential of ENTP Friendship

Underneath the bravado and sometimes unintentional prickliness, ENTPs have huge hearts. We're fiercely loyal, always ready to brainstorm solutions to your problems, and the most entertaining companions on life's weird adventures.

When we find friends who accept our need for both intellectual stimulation and occasional solitude, who appreciate our offbeat humor and genuine care, those friendships become some of the most vibrant and rewarding relationships in our lives.

"BORED" IS OUR FOUR-LETTER WORD: FINDING STIMULATION IN A PREDICTABLE WORLD

For most people, predictability is comforting. Routines create order, expectations set the stage for a smooth day. For ENTPs, predictability is the enemy. It's the creeping sensation that our brains are slowly mummifying, withering away from lack of novel input. We were born to explore, experiment, and push boundaries, and when life gets too routine-driven, we start to feel like caged animals.

Why ENTPs Crave Stimulation

It boils down to how our brains are wired:

- **Novelty seeking:** Extroverted Intuition (Ne), our dominant function, is always scanning for new patterns, possibilities, and potential. The unfamiliar lights us up; the known quickly loses its appeal.
- **Fast processing speeds:** ENTP minds take in and process information rapidly. When things are slow or repetitive, it's like running a Ferrari on a 25 mph road.
- **Love of learning:** We're naturally curious about the world and enjoy the challenge of wrapping our heads around new concepts or skills. Stagnation feels stifling.
- **Easily distracted:** Our attention is like a hyperactive puppy, easily drawn to anything that seems novel or interesting. This can make focusing on mundane tasks a Herculean feat.

What Boredom Feels Like for ENTPs

It's not just a mild "meh" feeling. ENTP boredom comes in several flavors:

- **Mental Fog:** That sluggish, uninspired state where your brain feels like it's filled with cotton wool.
- **Restlessness:** An inner itch to *do* something, anything, that might shake things up.
- **Irritability:** Snapping at people over minor things because everything feels unbearably irritating.
- **Existential Dread:** Those late-night bouts of "Is this all there is?" because life seems devoid of meaning and challenge.
- **Impulsivity:** Making rash decisions just to create some excitement—risky, but sometimes necessary.

Escaping the Boredom Trap: ENTP Strategies

1. The Constant Quest for Novelty
- **New hobbies:** Take a salsa class, learn basic coding, try your hand at improv. Variety is the spice of life for us.
- **Explore your environment:** Take a different route home, check out a new coffee shop, wander a neighborhood you've never visited ... small changes break the monotony.
- **Seek out interesting people:** Those with different perspectives, unusual careers, or fascinating life experiences provide fresh conversational fuel.
- **The 5-minute deep dive:** Got a random topic that tickles your fancy? Spend 5 minutes researching it. Satisfies the "shiny!" urge.

2. Turning the Ordinary into a Challenge
- **Gamify tasks:** Can you clean your room in record time? Turn grocery shopping into a treasure hunt?
- **Learn new skills within old tasks:** Got a boring presentation to give? Focus on mastering dynamic storytelling techniques.
- **Create mini-projects:** Redecorating on a budget? Turn it into a design challenge, complete with mood boards.

3. Mindset Shifts:

- **Reframe "Boring" as "Restorative":** If you're overstimulated, quiet time can be a chance to reset.
- **Boredom as a brainstorming signal:** When things feel slow, your subconscious might be working on a problem. Accept the lull, ideas may follow.

For ENTPs: Accepting Our Limits

Sometimes routine is unavoidable (hello, taxes!). It's about finding a balance – enough stimulation to keep our spark alive, but enough structure to actually function as adults.

For Those Around Us: Understanding the ENTP Need

- **Suggest novel experiences:** That quirky new restaurant, a thought-provoking documentary ... shows you understand them.
- **Accept our occasional restlessness:** It's not a reflection on you, it's how our brains function.
- **Don't be afraid to spice things up:** Surprise us with a random adventure or a thought experiment to kick off a stimulating conversation.

The Gift of a Stimulated ENTP

When we're not dying of boredom, ENTPs light up the world. We're more creative, more engaged, and more likely to share our infectious enthusiasm and outside-the-box ideas. A little effort to keep our minds buzzing goes a long way, both for us and the people lucky enough to be in our orbit.

THE ART OF THE ALMOST-FINISHED PROJECT: TAMING PROCRASTINATION

Raise your hand if you've got a collection of half-written essays, unfinished DIY projects, or abandoned business ideas gathering dust. Welcome to the ENTP procrastination club, where brilliant beginnings far outnumber completed works. It's not that we're lazy, it's that...well... things get complicated.

Why ENTPs are Procrastination Pros

1. The Thrill of the Start: The initial burst of inspiration is intoxicating. Brainstorming possibilities, outlining plans... it's all so exciting! The actual execution? Not so much.
2. Fear of Imperfection: With our broad knowledge and critical thinking skills, we see all the potential flaws in a project even before we start. This can be paralyzing.
3. Love of Novelty: Once the initial "shiny!" wears off, that unfinished project can't compete with the allure of a new idea.
4. Distractibility Supreme: Oh look, a YouTube video about the history of cheese! Goodbye work, hello random knowledge rabbit hole.
5. Thriving on Pressure: For some (crazy) ENTPs, the looming deadline is the only thing that triggers serious focus.

The Consequences of Chronic Procrastination

While we sometimes joke about our procrastination tendencies, it can have real downsides:

- Missed opportunities: Brilliance unexecuted means those great ideas stay trapped in our heads.
- Stress and guilt: The weight of unfinished projects creates a

constant background hum of anxiety.
- Damaged reputation: Flaking on commitments or constantly delivering work late erodes trust.
- Underachievement: We know we're capable of more, but procrastination holds us back.

Procrastination-Busting Strategies for ENTPs

1. Break it Down, Ridiculously Small:
- Instead of "Write novel," try "Write 200 words," or "Outline one character."
- Makes starting less daunting and builds momentum.

2. The "5-Minute Rule":
- Commit to just 5 minutes on the task. Often, once we start, we get into a flow state.
- If not, at least you put in a tiny bit of effort without the mental resistance.

3. Embrace "Good Enough":
- Perfectionism is our enemy. Aim for done, not perfect, especially with first drafts.
- You can always improve and polish later.

4. Accountability Buddies:
- Find someone who'll check on your progress (kindly, but firmly).
- Knowing someone's waiting for updates adds external motivation.

5. Reward Yourself:
- Build in rewards along the way, not just at the finish line.
- Finished a chapter? Treat yourself to that new video game or a fun outing.

6. The Pomodoro Technique:
- Work in focused bursts (25 mins on, 5 mins break) to combat

our distractible nature.

- Many apps help track your work/break sessions.

Additional Tips for ENTPs:

- **Recognize your patterns:** Do you procrastinate due to fear, boredom, or something else? This self-knowledge helps create tailored solutions.
- **Forgive yourself:** Beating yourself up makes it worse. Accept you're not perfect, then recommit to a slightly-better-than-yesterday approach.
- **Leverage hyperfocus:** When it occurs, harness that intense concentration to blast through a task.

Understanding Our Procrastination

ENTP procrastination isn't about laziness or lack of ability. It's a clash between our imaginative, possibility-loving minds and the need to execute in a linear, detail-oriented world.

However, by recognizing our tendencies and using strategies to outsmart them, we can start turning those brilliant ideas into reality.

The World Needs Completed ENTP Projects

So much amazing potential gets trapped within ENTP procrastination. Every project we finish – article written, business launched, skill mastered – is a gift, not just for ourselves, but for the world that benefits from our unique contributions.

WHY "FOCUS" FEELS LIKE
A DIRTY WORD

If you imagine the ENTP brain as a vibrant city square, focus becomes the equivalent of trying to hold a quiet meditation session in the middle of it all. There's a heated debate raging in one corner, a group of inventors excitedly sketching out a new contraption in another, a band unexpectedly bursts into song–oh, and is that a squirrel wearing a tiny hat? That's the ENTP mental landscape, where a million captivating distractions compete for our attention at any given moment.

Our superpower, Extroverted Intuition (Ne), is built for spotting connections, possibilities, and the grand scheme of things. It's what makes us brilliant at brainstorming, seeing patterns others miss, and adapting to changing situations with impressive speed. However, this also means traditional, linear focus is often our Achilles heel. We struggle to stay glued to a single task, especially when it feels mundane or detail-heavy, and those fascinating side trails that pop up along the way feel impossible to resist.

To make matters worse, ENTPs tend to crave novelty and stimulation. Our environment becomes a minefield: the sound of a passing car, an interesting notification, even our own internal musings can send us spiraling down an attention-sucking rabbit hole. This isn't just about having a short attention span; our brains are fundamentally wired for breadth rather than depth.

The consequences of our scattered focus can be frustratingly real. We might underperform when tasks require deep concentration, miss crucial details, or frustrate those around us with our topic-hopping tendencies. Long-term projects wither on the vine as our initial enthusiasm wanes, and we can't help but feel a pang of disappointment at our unfulfilled potential.

So, how do we tame the whirlwind? Here's the thing: ENTP focus will never look like that of a laser-focused specialist. Instead, we need strategies that work *with* our inherent nature, not against it. This might mean finding ways to channel our distractibility (scheduled breaks for those "shiny!" moments), creating a distraction-minimized workspace, breaking down tasks in ways that feel manageable, or finding ways to connect even dull work to our larger interests.

It's crucial for those in our lives to understand that our bouncing thought processes aren't a sign of disrespect, and with a little patience, our tangents might lead to valuable insights.

Ultimately, focus is a skill ENTPs can develop, just like building a muscle. It takes practice, self-awareness, and finding what works for *us*. When we do, harnessing our natural mental agility alongside a bit more focus makes us a force to be reckoned with.

ACCIDENTAL AWKWARDNESS: WHEN OUR MOUTH RUNS FASTER THAN OUR BRAIN

If you've ever witnessed an ENTP in full conversational flow, you know we have a unique talent for social interaction. We can be witty, insightful, and incredibly charming. But there's a dark side to this gift–a tendency to put our foot squarely in our mouths with mind-boggling regularity. It's not intentional... most of the time.

How ENTPs Achieve Peak Awkwardness

1.   Honesty Without a Filter: We value truth-telling and directness, sometimes forgetting that social interactions require a bit more...tact. Blunt observations that seem perfectly logical in our heads somehow cause awkward silence when uttered aloud.
2. Debating for Fun: When we see a statement, our first instinct is often to challenge it, explore its flaws, or play devil's advocate. What we think is intellectual playfulness can come across as combative or insensitive, particularly to those who take things more personally.
3.   The Curse of the Rapid-Fire Thought Train: Our brains process information quickly, leaping between ideas at a pace others can't follow. Out loud, this translates to jumping between seemingly unrelated topics, leaving conversational partners dazed and confused.
4.   Misreading Social Cues: Subtleties like facial expressions, body language, or tone of voice? We're often oblivious to these, especially when engrossed in an idea. This means we might miss signs that someone's uncomfortable or uninterested.
5.   Oversharing Vulnerability: Ironically, beneath the bravado,

ENTPs can be surprisingly open. We might blurt out deeply personal information when a fleeting sense of connection emboldens us, only to regret the overshare later.

Why This Matters

While sometimes humorous, our social clumsiness has consequences:

- Offended Friendships: A poorly-timed joke or overly blunt critique can hurt feelings, even if that wasn't our intention.
- Missed Opportunities: Awkward first impressions can hinder us from building relationships or networking successfully.
- Reputation Damage: If we're known for being unintentionally abrasive, people might avoid engaging with us.
- Self-Doubt: Even with thick skin, a string of awkward moments can make us second-guess ourselves.

Survival Strategies for Socially Awkward ENTPs

1. The Power of the Pause: Before speaking, take a nanosecond to ask: "Is this necessary? Is it kind? Is there a better way to phrase this?"
2. Observe and Learn: Pay attention to social cues. How do people react to different comments? This helps calibrate your conversational style.
3. Own the Awkwardness: Sometimes the best response is a lighthearted, "Whoops, that came out wrong," or "Classic case of my foot in my mouth!"
4. Empathy Development: Actively try to see things from others' perspectives. This helps predict how your words might land.
5. Your Superpower: Apologize sincerely. Most people understand ENTPs mean well, and a genuine apology goes a long way.

Tips for Those Who Love an ENTP

- Assume Positive Intent: We're usually not trying to be hurtful, just oblivious.
- Direct but Kind Feedback: Gently letting us know when we've overstepped is incredibly helpful.
- Don't Take it Personally: Our debate-loving tendencies are rarely about *you*.
- Appreciate the Authenticity: Beneath the occasional missteps, ENTPs bring a refreshingly honest energy to their interactions.

The Gift of the Gab

It's important to remember: our verbal mix of brilliance and blunder is a package deal. Our ability to spark lively conversations, cut through BS, and challenge norms is incredibly valuable, even if it comes with some bumps along the way.

By developing a bit more self-awareness and social fluency, ENTPs can minimize the awkwardness and maximize the positive impact of our natural communication style. After all, the world needs a little more unfiltered honesty and a healthy dose of humor, even if it comes with the occasional conversational cringe-fest.

EMOTIONAL INTELLIGENCE?
WE'RE WORKING ON IT...

If you've ever accused an ENTP of being a heartless robot, you're not entirely off-base. We're known for our intellectual prowess and logical analysis, but emotional intelligence isn't always our strong suit. It's not that we don't *have* feelings (we do, and they can be surprisingly intense), it's that processing emotions often sits low on our list of priorities.

Why ENTPs Struggle with the Emotional Realm

For starters, our dominant function, Extroverted Intuition (Ne), is focused on external possibilities, patterns, and connections, not our own internal landscape. We're wired to dissect ideas, not dwell on our feelings. On top of that, our secondary function, Introverted Thinking (Ti), is all about creating internal logical frameworks. It prioritizes accuracy and consistency, sometimes making emotions seem messy and irrational.

This combination can lead to some common ENTP blind spots:

- Difficulty Identifying Our Own Emotions: We might not have the vocabulary to articulate what we're feeling, instead describing it in intellectual terms or through physical sensations.
- Ignoring Emotions in Decision-Making: We favor logic and reason, often undervaluing the influence of our feelings until it leads to impulsive, emotionally-driven choices.
- Appearing Cold or Insensitive: Our focus on directness and our struggle to understand others' feelings can make us seem uncaring, even if that's far from the truth.
- Discomfort with Emotional Displays: Big emotional reactions can overwhelm us, leading to awkwardness or a tendency to intellectualize the situation rather than offering

support.

The Not-So-Hidden Depths

Here's the thing: ENTPs DO have rich inner emotional lives. We crave deep connection, get hurt like everyone else, and experience joy, love, and loss profoundly, even if we don't always show it in conventional ways. Our emotions often get channeled into our passions, fueling our creativity, determination, and unexpected moments of intense vulnerability.

Developing Emotional Maturity

Emotional intelligence, like any skill, can be improved with practice. For ENTPs, this means:

- Building Emotional Vocabulary: Learning to identify and name our feelings gives us more understanding and control over them.
- Embracing Vulnerability: Allowing ourselves to feel deeply, even when it's scary, unlocks connection and authenticity.
- Mindfulness Practices: Paying attention to our bodies and how emotions manifest physically helps us recognize them in real-time.
- Studying Human Behavior: Observing how others express emotions teaches us to recognize and interpret those feelings with more empathy.

The Benefits of Getting Emotionally Savvy

When ENTPs develop emotional intelligence, magic happens. We gain self-awareness, make better decisions that consider both logic *and* our values, build stronger, more honest relationships, and become more effective communicators overall. It's not about becoming someone we're not; it's about unlocking our full potential as well-rounded, emotionally intelligent humans.

For those interacting with ENTPs:

- Patience is Key: It takes time for us to develop emotional literacy.

- Ask Open-Ended Questions: "How did that make you feel?" encourages us to explore our emotions.
- Focus on the Intent: Our awkwardness rarely comes from malice, but from a genuine desire to understand.
- Be Direct: ENTPs appreciate clarity. Instead of getting upset, express your needs directly.

The world needs the ENTP blend of brilliance, passion, and authenticity. With a bit of work on our emotional intelligence, we can minimize the misunderstandings and maximize our positive impact on those around us.

FINDING YOUR TRIBE: PEOPLE WHO ACTUALLY GET YOU

As an ENTP, finding people who truly "get" you can feel like searching for a rare, mythical creature. We march to the beat of our own drum, crave deep intellectual stimulation, and have a knack for veering wildly off conversational tangents. This can make forging meaningful connections tricky, especially in a world that often values conformity and small talk.

Why ENTPs Crave a Different Kind of Connection

It's not that we don't enjoy people; we thrive on engaging interactions. However, our specific needs and quirks require a unique kind of social fuel:

- Intellectual Sparring Partners: We want someone who can keep up with our rapid-fire thoughts and challenges our ideas thoughtfully. Surface-level conversations leave us bored and disengaged.
- Embrace of the Weird: ENTPs need friends who find our random obsessions, offbeat humor, and tendency to passionately debate about the meaning of life fascinating, not odd.
- Honesty over Harmony: Directness and a willingness to dive into difficult topics are essential. We'd rather have a blunt truth than polite fluff.
- Patience for tangents: We need friends who don't roll their eyes when conversation veers from politics to existential philosophy to the best pizza toppings, all within 10 minutes.
- Appreciation for Enthusiasm (even Loud Enthusiasm): ENTPs get genuinely excited about ideas, and we need people who share, or at least tolerate, our sometimes boisterous expressiveness.

Where to Find Your People

The good news is, your tribe IS out there, you just need to know where to look:

- Interest-Based Communities: Seek out groups, whether online or in-person, focused on your niche passions. Whether it's a niche board game meetup or an online forum for astrophysics enthusiasts, shared interests are a strong starting point.
- Intellectual Hubs: Universities, think tanks, or even a lively local coffee shop can attract individuals who thrive on stimulating discussions.
- Personality-Based Groups: Online communities or local meet-up groups specifically for ENTPs or other intuitive types (INTJs, INFPs, INTPS) can be surprisingly validating and a source of genuine connection.
- Outside the Box: Don't underestimate the potential of unexpected places. You might find kindred spirits at a rock-climbing gym, a volunteer organization, or even in the comment section of an insightful blog post.

Cultivating Those Connections

Once found, these bonds require nurturing:

- Invest in the relationship: Deep connections take time, not just a single conversation fireworks display. Follow up, show interest in *their* passions, and find ways to continue the conversation.
- Reciprocity Matters: Be the kind of stimulating, supportive, and genuine friend you yourself seek out.
- Acceptance Is Key: Your tribe won't be perfect. Embrace their quirks, just as you expect them to embrace yours.

The Gift of a Like-Minded Community

Finding people who appreciate our brand of enthusiastic chaos is a game-changer for ENTPs. It fuels our creativity, reminds us we're not alone, provides endless opportunities for intellectual growth, and eases the loneliness that can come with feeling like the odd one out.

When we're surrounded by people who celebrate our quick wit, find our tangents endearing, and challenge us to think even deeper, we reach our fullest potential as ENTPs. So go forth, seek those who truly "get" you, and embrace the vibrant, stimulating, wonderfully weird tribe you deserve.

THE ENTP AND ROMANCE: A CONTRADICTION IN TERMS?

ENTPs in love are like a hurricane meeting a fireworks factory – thrilling, beautiful, and with a slight chance of everything exploding. We bring passion, intellectual spark, and a refreshingly unconventional approach to relationships. But our need for independence, analytical approach to emotions, and tendency to prioritize debate over harmony can create some unique challenges.

Why ENTP Romance Can Be Bumpy

- Craving Connection vs. Fear of Suffocation: ENTPs long for a deep, mind-melding level of connection, but also fiercely guard our autonomy. Navigating that balance can be tricky.
- Idealization vs. Reality: Our minds often paint a picture of the 'perfect' partner and relationship. When reality fails to match this (as it inevitably does), disillusionment can set in.
- Debate as Foreplay: Our love of lively discussion can be misinterpreted as argumentativeness or a lack of emotional investment, especially by partners who crave more overt affection.
- Emotional Unexpressiveness: While we have intense feelings, we often struggle to articulate them in traditional ways, leading to partners feeling neglected or unappreciated.
- The Boredom Monster: Routine and predictability are our kryptonite. Keeping the spark alive means continuously finding novelty and intellectual stimulation within the relationship.

The Upside of Loving an ENTP

We're far from hopeless romantics, but ENTPs bring a lot to the table:

- Fireworks and Fun: Life with an ENTP is rarely dull. We bring spontaneity, a playful sense of adventure, and a knack for making the ordinary extraordinary.
- Deeply Loyal (Once You're In): While we don't open up easily, those who earn our trust and respect have a fiercely devoted champion in their corner.
- Never-ending Intellectual Stimulation: We push our partners to grow, think critically, and see the world from fresh perspectives.
- Honesty and Openness: We don't play games. With an ENTP, you get upfront communication and a commitment to finding genuine solutions to problems.
- Constant Growth: We want our partners to thrive as individuals and will eagerly support their passions and personal goals.

Finding Love, the ENTP Way

For ENTPs to find fulfilling relationships, it takes both self-awareness and finding the right kind of partner. Here's the key:

- Seek an Intellectual Equal: Someone who loves to spar verbally, has their own fascinating interests, and challenges us is ideal.
- Open Communication is Crucial: A partner who expresses their needs clearly and isn't afraid of honest, sometimes difficult, conversations is a must.
- Independence as an Asset: We need partners who respect our need for alone time and don't see it as a personal rejection.
- Embrace the Weirdness: We'll never be traditional romantics. Someone who finds our quirks charming rather than confusing is perfect.

Tips for Loving an ENTP

- Challenge Us: Don't let us get away with intellectual laziness; engage in lively debates.
- Initiate Novelty: Spontaneous adventures, surprise gifts of

the "weird but fascinating" variety keep us engaged.

- Honesty is King/Queen: Tell us directly what you need, we appreciate clarity over hinting.
- Space is Love: Respecting our occasional need for solitude actually strengthens the connection.
- Celebrate Our Growth: When we make an effort to express emotions or work on our romantic blind spots, show appreciation for the effort.

The ENTP relationship adventure won't always be smooth sailing, but with the right partner, it's a wild, exhilarating ride. We offer a love that's stimulating, unconventional, and forever evolving. If you're up for the challenge, the rewards are more than worth it.

WORK LIFE: WHEN STRUCTURE IS THE ENEMY, AND BRILLIANCE CAN BE CONFUSING

The traditional workplace can feel like a cage for the ENTP mind. Craving freedom, autonomy, and constant intellectual stimulation, we can easily clash with the constraints of rigid routines, mind-numbing tasks, and the oh-so-frustrating pace of bureaucracy. However, ENTPs have unique strengths that, when recognized and harnessed, make us invaluable assets to any team.

ENTP Workplace Struggles

- The 9 to 5 Grind: Routine schedules, repetitive tasks, and sitting through endless pointless meetings are like torture devices designed to drain our motivation. We need variety and challenge to stay engaged.
- Office Politics: We're wired to question everything and gravitate towards truth over harmony. This can make us seem confrontational or uncooperative when navigating office dynamics.
- Hierarchical Constraints: Authority for the sake of authority irks us. We respect competence, not just a title, and don't hesitate to challenge decisions that seem illogical.
- Uninspiring Work: If tasks don't spark our curiosity or offer room for creative problem-solving, we quickly check out. Our brains crave continual stimulation and learning.

The Untapped ENTP Potential in the Workplace

- Innovators and Problem-Solvers: We see connections others miss, question assumptions, and thrive on finding unconventional solutions. This makes us natural innovators and troubleshooters.

- Strategic Thinkers: Our ability to see the big picture and spot patterns makes us valuable for strategic planning and identifying potential opportunities or threats.
- Excellent Communicators (When We Care): When fully engaged, we have a gift for explaining complex ideas in clear, compelling ways. This is a major asset for client-facing roles or internal team leadership.
- Energizing Forces: Our natural enthusiasm can be infectious. We inject excitement into projects and motivate those around us to think outside the box.
- Change Agents: We don't just accept the status quo; we're constantly seeking ways to improve systems and increase efficiency.

Finding Our Workplace Niche

ENTPs thrive in environments that allow for:

- Autonomy and Ownership: Micromanagement is our nemesis. Trust us with a goal, provide necessary resources, and get out of the way.
- Problem-Solving Focus: Jobs that involve tackling new challenges, analyzing complex systems, or strategizing solutions play to our strengths.
- Flexibility and Variety: Rigid structures stifle us. We need flexibility in scheduling or the opportunity to work on multiple, diverse projects.
- Room for Idea Generation: Companies that value innovation and encourage employees to share their "what if?" moments are where we shine.
- Intellectual Comradeship: While we enjoy independence, having colleagues who 'get' us and engage in stimulating discussions fuels our best work.

Tips for Thriving as an ENTP Employee

- Find Your Advocates: Seek out managers or mentors who appreciate your unique talents and can champion your ideas.

- Negotiate When Possible: Can't avoid some tasks? Negotiate to work on them during your peak energy hours or propose ways to increase their complexity.
- Reframe Boring Tasks: Find a way to connect even mundane work to a larger goal or a chance to improve a system.
- Self-Employment: If traditional structures feel unbearable, entrepreneurship might be your calling, allowing you to set your own rules and direction.

For Employers: Getting the Best from ENTPs

- Challenge Us: Don't just give tasks, frame them as problems to be solved with unique solutions.
- Focus on Results, Not Process: If we find a faster, more effective way to get the job done, who cares if it's unconventional?
- Provide Mentorship: Pair ENTPs with experienced colleagues who can offer guidance, especially with navigating workplace politics.
- Offer Learning Opportunities: Support for continuing education or the chance to learn new skills keeps us motivated.
- Value Our Input: Create channels for ENTPs to share ideas and suggestions for improvement.

The ENTP work life dance involves understanding our unique needs and proactively finding ways to channel our brilliance (while minimizing the potential for office-rule-breaking chaos). We defy the standard worker-drone model, but in the right setting, we're a force of innovation and progress for any organization.

THE GIFT OF GAB: WHEN TALKING IS AN OLYMPIC SPORT

If conversations were a competitive event, ENTPs would be training for the gold medal. We're natural-born conversationalists, fueled by a love of ideas, unquenchable curiosity, and a sometimes startling ability to leap from one topic to the next at a pace that leaves others breathless.

Why ENTPs Love to Talk

- Idea Exploration: Talking is thinking out loud for us. It's how we process information, make connections, and refine our thoughts.
- The Thrill of Debate: We enjoy a good intellectual sparring match. Poking holes in arguments, playing devil's advocate, and exploring different perspectives is like a mental sport.
- Sharing Knowledge: If we've learned something fascinating, we're bursting to share it. Our enthusiasm can be contagious, sparking interesting discussions.
- Pattern Seekers: We make connections between seemingly unrelated things. Talking allows us to trace those threads, sometimes uncovering surprising insights.
- Genuine Connection: Despite our love of debate, ENTPs crave connection. Conversation is a way to learn about others, discover common ground, and forge strong bonds.

The Accidental Monologue: When Our Gift Goes Awry

Our conversational exuberance, however, can sometimes backfire:

- Tangent Overload: Our mental leaps can leave listeners lost. We start talking about space travel, suddenly veer into the economics of the banana industry, and somehow land on the symbolism of squirrels in Renaissance art.

- Dominating the Conversation: Without realizing it, our enthusiasm can turn into a one-person show, leaving others struggling to get a word in.
- Conversational Intensity: We can come across as too blunt, argumentative, or intellectually intimidating, especially for those who prefer a gentler conversational pace.
- Misreading Cues: Focused on the idea, we might miss signs that someone's bored, confused, or ready to change the subject.

Taming the Talking Beast: Tips for ENTPs

- Embrace the Pause: Before launching into a thought, take a moment to ask yourself: Is this relevant to the current discussion? Will it interest others?
- Listen, Really Listen: Pay attention to your conversational partner. Their expressions, body language, and responses provide vital clues to whether you're on the right track.
- Ask Open-Ended Questions: Shift some conversational responsibility onto others. This shows genuine interest and creates space for them to contribute.
- Set Internal Timers: Challenge yourself to keep your initial responses or monologues to a set time limit.
- Self-deprecation is Your Friend: A little humor about your tendency to ramble ("Oops, there I go on a tangent again!") eases any awkwardness.

For Those Conversing with an ENTP:

- Ask Questions: Dig deeper into what intrigues us, guiding our scattered thoughts to a more focused exploration.
- Redirect Gently: "That's super interesting, but let's circle back to..." brings us back on track without quashing our enthusiasm.
- It's Not Personal: Our debating style is about the idea, not attacking you. Let us know if it ever feels too intense.
- Appreciate the Entertainment Value: Sometimes leaning back and enjoying our wild thought trajectories is the best

approach.

The Power of a Well-Harnessed ENTP Chat

When we become more aware of our conversational tendencies and others learn to navigate our enthusiastic style, the ENTP gift of gab truly shines. We bring a level of energy, humor, and intellectualism to conversations that few other types can match.

The best conversations with an ENTP are like an exhilarating roller coaster ride: twists, turns, surprising drops, and moments where you just throw your hands up and laugh. At the end of it, you're left buzzing with a sense of possibility, having explored ideas you'd never have considered on your own.

MASTER STRATEGISTS (OR ARE WE JUST WINGING IT?)

Whether it's plotting a global takeover (just kidding...probably), devising the perfect plan for a weekend getaway, or mapping out an epic argument against the absurdity of wearing socks with sandals, ENTPs have a knack for strategy. Our ability to see the big picture, weave together disparate information, and envision multiple possibilities makes us natural schemers and plotters.

The ENTP Strategic Mind

1. Pattern Spotters: We see connections and underlying patterns that others miss. This allows us to anticipate potential problems, spot opportunities, and understand the complex interplay of different factors in a situation.
2. Scenario Builders: Our minds can rapidly generate multiple scenarios ("If we do this, X might happen, but that could lead to Y or Z"). This allows us to anticipate and plan across various outcomes.
3. Improvisational Brilliance: While we enjoy planning, we're at our best when things go awry. ENTPs thrive on adapting quickly, finding creative solutions on the fly, and turning setbacks into unexpected advantages.
4. Systems Thinkers: We don't just address the immediate issue, we analyze the entire system it exists within. This allows us to create more comprehensive strategies and identify potential leverage points.

Where Our Strategic Skills Shine

- Problem-Solving: When faced with a complex challenge, ENTPs see it like a multi-dimensional puzzle. We enjoy breaking it down, finding unconventional solutions, and anticipating roadblocks.

- Project Planning: Our ability to visualize the big picture and spot potential pitfalls makes us valuable for project planning and identifying necessary resources.
- Long-Term Visioning: We're not just focused on the immediate task, but always considering how it fits into larger goals, both personal and organizational.
- Debate and Persuasion: ENTPs are natural strategists when arguing a point. We anticipate counterarguments, find flaws in logic, and plot conversational moves to gain the upper hand.

The Illusion of Having Our Act Together

The truth is, sometimes we're superbly organized planners, and other times, we're brilliantly improvising our way through chaos. Here's the ENTP strategy paradox:

- Action vs. Planning: We often want to dive into action before having every detail mapped out. The plan might be a little hazy, but we trust in our ability to figure it out along the way.
- Procrastination-Fueled Brilliance: That looming deadline? For some ENTPs, it's the catalyst for unparalleled focus and strategic thinking.
- Flexibility as a Core Strategy: Rigidity is our enemy. Our best-laid plans include built-in room for change, because we know unexpected opportunities or obstacles will undoubtedly arise.

Tips for ENTP Strategists

- Capture the Big Picture First: Before diving into details, outline the overall goal and the major steps required to get there.
- Force Yourself to Prioritize: Not every potential scenario needs in-depth analysis. Identify the most crucial elements to focus your planning energy.
- Find Your Planning Medium: Mind maps, flowcharts, or even quick sketches can help visualize complex strategies and

keep you on track.

- Delegate When Possible: We're great at the vision, but sometimes others are better at the detail-oriented execution.

For Collaborators:

- Don't Expect a Step-by-Step Plan (At First): Focus on the big picture goal and trust the ENTP to fill in the blanks, often brilliantly on the fly.
- Challenge Our Assumptions: Ask questions to ensure we've considered potential blind spots or unintended consequences.
- Appreciate the Adaptability: If Plan A fails, trust that the ENTP is already working on Plan B, C, and possibly even D.

Whether we're meticulous architects or chaotic whirlwinds with a surprising success rate, ENTPs bring a unique strategic edge to the table. With a bit of self-awareness and (occasional) discipline, we can harness our planning powers to achieve extraordinary results.

OVERTHINKING EVERYTHING: OUR BRAINS' FAVORITE HOBBY

If overthinking were an Olympic event, ENTPs would be undisputed champions. Our minds are relentless thought-generating machines, zooming in on details, unraveling possibilities, analyzing arguments, and reliving past conversations – often all at the same time. It's a superpower with a self-destructive streak.

The ENTP Overthinking Experience

1. The Infinite "What If?" Loop: Every decision, past event, or new piece of information triggers an onslaught of analysis. What if I'd said this differently? What if this project fails? What if the true meaning of existence is...pizza?
2. Magnifying the Negatives: Our brains have a pesky habit of fixating on what *could* go wrong, past mistakes, or potential criticisms, making minor issues seem catastrophic.
3. Mental Rehearsals Gone Wild: We rehash conversations obsessively, re-playing them with various alternative responses to find the "perfect" thing we should have said.
4. Analysis Paralysis: Overthinking can leave us frozen, unable to make even simple decisions because the sheer number of potential outcomes feels overwhelming.
5. Emotional Rollercoaster: The constant mental chatter takes a toll. It leads to anxiety, doubt, insomnia, and prevents us from enjoying the present moment.

Why Our Brains Betray Us

- Extroverted Intuition Overload: Our dominant function (Ne) is designed to spot possibilities. Unfortunately, it doesn't discriminate between the positive and catastrophic ones.
- Fear of Failure (or worse, Boredom): We want to make the

optimal choice, avoid mistakes, or find the most stimulating path – overthinking is a misguided attempt to ensure this.

- Unresolved Issues: ENTPs value internal logical consistency. If something doesn't make sense, we'll obsess over it until we've (over)analyzed it into submission.

Taming the Thought Tornado

1. Mindfulness Techniques: Bringing conscious awareness to the present moment helps break the overthinking spiral. Meditation, deep breathing, or focusing intently on a simple task can provide a much-needed mental reset.
2. Questioning Your Thoughts: Are these thoughts productive? Are they realistic? Challenging the negative thought loops helps reduce their control over you.
3. Time-Limited Worry Sessions: Give yourself a set amount of time (say 15 minutes) to fully indulge the overthinking. Once done, move on to something else.
4. Action as an Antidote: Instead of endlessly analyzing, take a small step towards whatever you're overthinking. Break the paralysis by doing *something.*
5. Embracing Imperfection: Accept that mistakes are part of growth, and not every decision needs to be the "perfect" one. Sometimes, done is better than perfect.

Additional Tips for ENTPs:

- Physical Exercise: Getting your body moving can quiet the mental chatter.
- Journaling: Putting your swirling thoughts on paper makes them less overwhelming.
- Talk to Someone: Sometimes an outside perspective from a trusted friend can help break the overthinking loop.

For Those Who Love Us:

- Be Patient and Reassuring: Let us verbalize our worries without judgment or trying to "fix" everything immediately.
- Distraction Can Help: Suggesting a change of activity,

whether it's a walk or a silly game, can provide a needed mental break.

- Don't Minimize Our Concerns: Acknowledge the struggle, even if the overthinking seems irrational from the outside.

The Gift of a Balanced ENTP Mind

When tamed (not entirely eliminated, because let's be real), our powerful analytical skills are an asset. We're strategic problem solvers, able to anticipate pitfalls, and create ingenious solutions.

Finding the balance between harnessing our mental acuity and not letting it drive us into a frenzy is a lifelong practice for the ENTP. But with awareness and some strategies to break the spiral, we can use our amazing minds for good, not self-induced torture.

REBELS WITH A CAUSE: CHALLENGING THE NORM

ENTPs are the rebellious spirits of the personality type world. We don't follow rules just for the sake of it, question authority just because it's there, and have an uncanny ability to spot flaws, inconsistencies, and outright BS in any system. It's not about being contrary for the sake of it; it's about a deep-seated drive for truth, efficiency, and a world that just makes logical sense.

Why We Rebel

1. An Allergy to Inefficiency: When something is slow, illogical, or serves no clear purpose, our brains itch to fix it. Traditions or procedures simply because "that's how we've always done it" drive us mad.
2. In Love With Progress: We see potential for improvement everywhere. Stagnation feels suffocating, and we're constantly asking "What if we tried a better way?"
3. Independence is Oxygen: ENTPs crave autonomy. When rules feel arbitrary or limit our ability to think and act freely, our rebellious streak flares up.
4. Playing Devil's Advocate is Our Default Mode: We question everything, not out of malice, but out of a genuine desire to understand the why behind things and test if ideas can withstand scrutiny.
5. Bored by the Status Quo: Rules and traditions can feel stifling to our possibility-seeking minds. Routine for its own sake makes us want to shake things up.

The Positive Side of the ENTP Rebel

While we might frustrate those who value strict order and adherence to tradition, our rebellious nature serves a valuable purpose:

- Innovation Catalysts: We push boundaries, refusing to accept "that's impossible." This often leads to breakthroughs and novel solutions.
- Defenders of Logic: We call out bad policies, flawed arguments, and outdated systems, forcing important improvements.
- Champions of the Underdog: ENTPs see potential where others see limitations, and we're willing to fight for those who are overlooked or treated unfairly.
- Guardians of Individuality: We remind people that blind conformity isn't a virtue and that it's okay (and actually beneficial) to think for yourself.

When Our Rebellion Goes Too Far

Sometimes our zeal for questioning norms can backfire:

- Alienating Others: Being constantly contrarian just for the fun of it erodes trust and makes others less receptive to our valid critiques.
- Impulsive Rebellions: If we leap into action before fully thinking through the consequences or building support, our attempts at change can fizzle out.
- Missing the Big Picture: While we're great at spotting flaws, we sometimes lose sight of the potential benefits of stability that rules and systems can provide.

Tips for Constructive ENTP Rebellion

1. Pick Your Battles Wisely: Not every rule deserves to be broken. Focus your rebellious energy on things that genuinely matter and where you believe you can make a real difference.
2. Understand the Opposition: Before launching a rebellious campaign, learn why the rule or system exists. There may be reasons you haven't considered.
3. Build Alliances: Change is more likely to happen if you have support. Find like-minded people who share your concerns.

4.   Offer Solutions, Not Just Critiques: Simply tearing something down makes you an agitator, not a change-maker. Present well-thought-out alternatives.

5.   Channel Your Inner Diplomat (Sometimes): A bit of tact can go a long way. Express your critiques constructively and respectfully, even when it feels painful to do so.

For Those Dealing with Rebellious ENTPs

- Recognize Our Intent: Most of the time, we're trying to make things better, not just be difficult.
- Listen to the 'Why': Beneath the challenge, there's often a valid idea or concern. Separate the delivery style from the content.
- Offer a Chance to Lead: Let the ENTP propose solutions or head up a committee to improve problematic systems. This channels their energy productively.
- Value the Outside Perspective: We highlight things others have become blind to, even if delivered in a less-than-ideal package.

ENTPs are a force for progress when we balance our rebellious instincts with strategy and a bit of understanding for the less change-enthusiastic humans among us. We're the ones who dare to ask the uncomfortable questions, challenge the established order, and relentlessly push for a world that lives up to its full potential.

HARNESSING THE CHAOS: PRODUCTIVITY HACKS FOR THE SCATTERBRAINED

ENTPs are notorious for our scattered minds, boundless energy, and a propensity to leave a trail of half-started projects in our wake. However, the illusion of chaos hides a desire for accomplishment – if we could just get those brilliant ideas out of our heads and into reality.

Traditional productivity systems often don't resonate with our unique mental wiring. The good news is, with some non-traditional tweaks and experimentation, ENTPs can become productivity powerhouses.

Challenge #1: Procrastination Is Our Middle Name

- Beat Procrastination by Gamifying: Turn boring tasks into challenges. Time yourself, or compete with a friend to inject some much-needed urgency.
- Embrace the Mini-Project: Reframe daunting tasks as a series of short, focused bursts. It's less overwhelming and provides those dopamine hits we crave.
- Harness the Power of Deadlines: Even artificial ones. Tell a friend about your goal or publicly declare it to create some external pressure.

Challenge #2: We're Idea Magnets (and Easily Distracted by Shiny Ones)

- Brain Dump Station: Designate a specific "idea catch" space – a notebook, a notetaking app, or a dedicated whiteboard. Jot it down FAST and return to your main task.
- Time-Box the Shiny: When distraction strikes, give yourself 15 minutes max to indulge, then ruthlessly return to your

priority.

- Change Your Environment: Distracting setting? Relocate often. Library, coffee shop, a park bench – variety can help focus.

Challenge #3: Routine Makes Us Break Out In Hives

- Build Flexibility INTO Your Routine: Schedule blocks of "focus time" but have a few options on what to work on within those blocks to retain some autonomy.
- Micro-Routines: Instead of rigid daily schedules, build small, easy-to-follow routines within tasks (ie. how you start writing projects).
- Prioritize by Excitement: Which task sparks the most interest RIGHT NOW? Ride that wave of motivation while it lasts.

Additional ENTP Productivity Hacks

- Find Your Time: Are you a night owl or an early bird? Schedule focus work during your peak energy hours.
- Accountability Partners: Find a supportive friend or group who understand your working style and will provide gentle nudges when needed.
- Visualize the Outcome: Connect tasks to your big-picture goals. This makes the mundane feel more meaningful.
- Celebrate the Wins: Acknowledging even small successes fuels our motivation and keeps us from feeling overwhelmed.
- Tech Tools, BUT Carefully: Productivity apps can be amazing or another rabbit hole. Experiment, find what works, then stick with a few essentials.

Productivity Is NOT about Becoming Someone You're Not

It's about embracing our chaotic-creative wiring while developing some strategies that support our natural strengths instead of fighting against them. Here's the thing to remember:

- Consistency Is the Enemy: Expect fluctuations in productivity and forgive yourself for the off days.
- Done Is Better Than Perfect (Usually): Aim for progress, not some unattainable ideal of linear perfection.
- Rest Is Productive: Recharge time is crucial for ENTP brains to process, consolidate, and come up with the next brilliant idea.

For the ENTP, productivity is an ongoing experiment. Some days we'll be unstoppable, others we'll stare at a blank page for hours. The key is self-awareness, a willingness to try new strategies, and a good dose of humor to cope with the inevitable moments of spectacular derailment.

FINDING OUR NICHE: WHEN PASSION MEETS POTENTIAL

ENTPs have the potential to excel in numerous fields, but finding the "perfect" career path can be a lifelong quest. Our thirst for challenge, novelty, and intellectual stimulation means that soul-sucking jobs with repetitive tasks and rigid hierarchies are a recipe for professional misery. So, where does our unique blend of brilliance and scattered enthusiasm actually thrive?

The ENTP Ideal Workplace

For ENTPs to reach their full potential, they need a workplace that offers a few key elements:

- Problem-Solving Focus: We shine brightest when tackling complex challenges that require strategic thinking, innovative solutions, and the ability to see connections others miss. Positions that involve constant learning and opportunities to break new ground are ideal.
- Autonomy and Flexibility: Micromanagement is an ENTP's kryptonite. We need the trust to manage our own time, explore different approaches, and have flexibility in our work schedule if possible.
- Intellectual Comradeship: While we're independent thinkers, having colleagues who match our intellectual curiosity fuels us. We thrive in environments that foster collaboration, lively discussion, and the sharing of ideas.
- Recognition of Potential: ENTPs need to feel that our unique talents are valued and that opportunities for growth exist. We wither in environments where we feel stagnant or pigeonholed.

Career Paths Where ENTPs Flourish

There's no one-size-fits-all career for an ENTP. However, some fields repeatedly rise to the top of fulfilling ENTP professions:

- Entrepreneurship: The ultimate playground for our independent spirits, love of problem-solving, and knack for spotting possibilities. Building something from the ground up allows us to exercise all our strengths and control our own destiny.
- Technology and Innovation: Fast-paced fields like software development, data science, or UX design offer endless intellectual challenges, opportunities for innovative solutions, and the chance to be at the forefront of progress.
- Research and Analysis: Whether in academia, a think tank, or market research, ENTPs excel in roles that require digging into complex information, uncovering patterns, and developing actionable insights.
- Law or Policy: Our debating skills and ability to see all sides of an issue can be a huge asset. Positions in advocacy, patent law, or policy development allow us to fight for ideas we believe in and create meaningful change.
- Creative Fields with Problem-Solving Elements: ENTPs can thrive as strategists in marketing, filmmakers tackling complex themes, or game designers creating intricate, immersive experiences.

Signs You've Found Your Niche

Aside from the obvious feeling of "this doesn't completely suck", here's how to know you're on the right track:

- Flow State: You lose track of time because you're so engrossed in your work.
- It Doesn't Feel Like Work: You're genuinely excited about challenges and find yourself thinking about work projects even outside office hours (in a good way).
- Learning & Growth: You're constantly developing new skills and expanding your knowledge base.

- Energy, Not Burnout: While exhaustion is inevitable sometimes, you feel energized by your work on most days.

Overcoming ENTP Career Obstacles

Even in promising fields, ENTPs still face challenges. Self-awareness and a few strategies can help:

- Communicate Your Value: ENTPs don't always fit the traditional mold, so clearly articulating how our unique skills solve problems for the company is crucial.
- Channel the Enthusiasm: Passion is an asset, but make sure it's not coming across as chaotic or scattered. Practice concisely summarizing your ideas.
- Build Focus Muscles: Finding ways to stay on track with larger projects (break them down, set mini-deadlines) will showcase our incredible ability to execute.

Sometimes, the most fulfilling ENTP path is the one we carve ourselves. Freelancing, consulting, or starting side projects allows us to tailor our work experiences, embrace variety, and play to our ever-evolving strengths. The key is to keep experimenting, learning, pushing our boundaries, and remembering that the journey towards a fulfilling career is a lifelong adventure, not a straight and narrow path.

BURNOUT AND THE ENTP: LEARNING WHEN TO HIT PAUSE

ENTPs thrive on energy, possibility, and the thrill of tackling new challenges. But our relentless enthusiasm and drive can be a double-edged sword. We're prone to a particular kind of burnout – a fizzling out of our internal spark that leaves us feeling uncharacteristically flat, cynical, and mentally exhausted.

Why ENTPs Are Susceptible to Burnout

- The Hamster Wheel of Ideas: Our brains are constantly whirring, generating ideas, questioning assumptions, and seeking stimulation. This can lead to mental overload and a feeling of never being able to fully shut off.
- Ignoring Our Need for Recharge: We can get so caught up in exciting projects or debates that we neglect basic self-care, sacrificing sleep, healthy habits, and downtime in the name of productivity.
- Boredom Disguised as Burnout: Routine, repetitive tasks, and unchallenging environments can sap our energy. We may misinterpret this soul-crushing boredom as burnout.
- Emotional Intensity Suppression: If we feel pressured to constantly be the "rational" ones, suppressing our sometimes intense feelings can take a toll over time.
- The Pressure to Perform: Our drive for success, coupled with a tendency towards perfectionism, can make it hard to acknowledge when we're reaching our limits.

Signs an ENTP is Burning Out

Unlike the stereotypical image of burnout as complete collapse, ENTP burnout often looks like this:

- Loss of Enthusiasm: Things that normally excite you feel

dull and pointless.

- Increased Cynicism: That usual optimistic spark is replaced by snark and a negative outlook on everything.
- Mental Fog: It's hard to concentrate, ideas that flowed effortlessly feel stuck, and decision-making becomes agonizing.
- Irritability and Impatience: You snap at loved ones, lose your cool over minor things, and feel a general simmering frustration.
- Questioning Everything: It's more than just a bad day. You find yourself in an existential funk, doubting your path, your abilities, and the point of it all.

The Danger of Ignoring the Warning Signs

ENTPs are excellent at rationalizing away exhaustion. If we don't hit the pause button, burnout can have serious consequences:

- Diminished Potential: Our ability to think creatively, problem-solve, and see the big picture becomes compromised.
- Relationship Strain: Burnout makes us less patient, less present, and more likely to lash out at those closest to us.
- Physical Health Impact: Prolonged stress and lack of self-care can weaken our immune system and increase the risk of health problems.
- Full-Blown Existential Crisis: If ignored long enough, ENTP burnout can lead to a complete loss of direction and questioning our fundamental identity.

Recharging, Not Refueling: Strategies for ENTPs

1. Recognize the Signs: Pay attention to those subtle burnout signals and don't dismiss them as mere moodiness.
2. Radical Rest: This means not just sleep, but activities that truly replenish you, whether it's mindless entertainment, time in nature, or turning off devices for a digital detox.
3. Embrace "Good Enough": Temporarily lower your standards.

Delegate what you can, and focus on essentials to free up mental space.

4. Sensory Change-Up: Blast music and dance like a maniac, try a new cuisine, or get a massage. Engages our senses that are dulled from mental overload.

5.   Talk it Out: Find a trusted friend or therapist to process frustrations without the need to be the "rational, upbeat" one.

Reframing Burnout for ENTPs

Think of it as an internal warning system that something's not aligned. It's a chance to:

- Reassess Priorities: Are you pouring energy into projects that truly matter to you, or getting sidetracked by less meaningful obligations?
- Explore New Territory: Burnout could be a sign that you need a bigger challenge or to tap into a neglected interest.
- Build Self-Care Habits: Burnout forces us to acknowledge we're not invincible. Use it as a catalyst to develop sustainable habits that support long-term energy.

Most importantly, remember burnout is not a sign of weakness or failure. It's a sign that you're an ambitious, passionate human with finite resources. Learning to recognize our limits and integrating intentional periods of rest and recalibration is actually the key to sustaining our long-term drive and unlocking our full, brilliant, slightly chaotic potential as an ENTP.

TAPPING INTO OUR HIDDEN DEPTHS: THE SENSITIVE SIDE OF ENTPS

Think of the stereotypical ENTP, and "sensitive" probably isn't the adjective that springs to mind. We're the debaters, the innovators, the ones who seem emotionally unflappable while engaging in the intellectual equivalent of gladiatorial combat. But beneath the bravado and quick wit, ENTPs have surprisingly deep emotional wells. We may not wear our hearts on our sleeves, but that doesn't mean they aren't there.

The Paradox of the ENTP Feelers

Our dominant function, Extroverted Intuition (Ne), focuses on external possibilities and patterns. Our second function, Introverted Thinking (Ti), prioritizes internal logic. This combination leads to a unique approach to emotions:

- We Think, Then Feel: Our initial response to situations is often analytical. We dissect problems, seek solutions, and only later do the corresponding emotions catch up.
- Awkward Vulnerability: Expressing deep emotions outwardly can feel clunky and unnatural. We may downplay them or intellectualize them, even to ourselves.
- Intensity Behind the Scenes: ENTPs DO feel deeply. But we process these emotions privately. Joy, hurt, anger – these flare up intensely, then get tucked away for analysis.
- Seeking Meaning in Emotion: We're not content to just feel. We need to understand why we feel, connect it to our values, and derive insights for personal growth.
- Hypersensitivity to Injustice: Witnessing unfairness, cruelty, or the undermining of potential can trigger powerful emotional responses in an ENTP.

Why This Matters

Recognizing our emotional complexity helps us develop greater self-awareness, build stronger relationships, and unlock new aspects of our potential. When we dismiss our emotional side, we end up with:

- Frustration in Relationships: Those close to us may feel we're uncaring or cold when we struggle to articulate our feelings in conventional ways.
- Suppressed Intensity = Eventual Explosion: If we bottle up emotions too long, they leak out as bursts of anger or unexpected deep sadness.
- Missed Opportunities for Connection: Our ability to empathize is underrated. Denying our feelings blocks us from forging genuine bonds based on shared human experiences.

Embracing Our Emotional Depths: ENTP Style

Developing emotional fluency doesn't mean turning into a completely different personality type. It's about honoring this aspect of ourselves, even if it feels a bit uncomfortable at first. Here's how:

- Build Emotional Vocabulary: Learning to identify and name our emotions gives us more control over them, instead of them surprising us later.
- Observe and Analyze: Pay attention to your body's reactions in emotional situations. What are the physical sensations connected to different feelings?
- Find Safe Outlets: Journaling, therapy, or confiding in a trusted friend provides space to process emotions without judgment.
- Embrace the Nuance: Emotions aren't always black or white. We can feel frustrated yet optimistic, heartbroken yet hopeful – allow for complexity.
- Express in Our Own Way: Heartfelt speeches may not be our

jam. Share emotions through actions, a well-chosen piece of music, or a written note when words fail.

The Benefits of Feeling Deeply

When ENTPs tap into their emotional depths, they become a force to be reckoned with. It unlocks:

- Stronger Relationships: When we can express vulnerability and empathy, it deepens the trust and connection we share with others.
- Enhanced Problem-Solving: Emotions provide valuable data about our values and priorities, leading to more well-rounded solutions.
- Greater Authenticity: Embracing the full spectrum of who we are reduces internal dissonance and allows our true selves to shine through.
- Fuel for Our Passions: Deep emotions, whether positive or negative, serve as a powerful motivator for fighting for what we believe in.

For Others in an ENTP's Life

- Patience is Key: It takes time for us to trust others with our emotional side. Don't expect instant gushes of feeling.
- Focus on Actions: We may show love through solving problems, acts of service, or sharing something that made us think of you.
- Ask Open-Ended Questions: "How did that make you feel?" opens more doors for deeper emotional sharing than a direct "Are you okay?".
- Respecting Our Need to Process: We may need time and space to grapple with emotions before we can articulate them clearly.

ENTPs are a unique blend of intellectual brilliance and unexpected depth. While logic is our native language, embracing our emotional side adds rich new layers to our personalities. When we allow ourselves to feel deeply, we can form stronger connections, become more well-rounded problem solvers, and tap into reserves of passion that make us an unstoppable force for positive change in the world.

64

SELF-ACCEPTANCE: EMBRACING OUR WEIRD AND WONDERFUL

If ENTPs had a coat of arms, it would feature a question mark emblazoned over a jester juggling flaming squirrels. We're a delightful contradiction: brilliant yet scatterbrained, social yet fiercely independent, and prone to questioning the absurdity of existence while passionately debating the optimal toppings for pizza. Self-acceptance, for us, isn't a fluffy, feel-good concept – it's the key to unlocking our full, chaotic potential.

Why ENTPs Struggle with Self-Acceptance

- The Curse of High Standards: Our minds are idea factories. We're constantly envisioning all the ways we could be better, smarter, more accomplished. This makes it easy to fall into the trap of always focusing on what we lack, not what we are.
- Social Misfits: We don't fit neatly into boxes. Our off-beat humor, unusual interests, and tendency to switch conversational gears with abandon can make us feel like oddballs.
- Fear of Boring Normality: Deep down, ENTPs fear becoming a predictable cog in the machine of society. This can lead to rejecting any hint of conformity, even when it's in healthy ways.
- Emotional Blind Spots: Our discomfort with emotions can translate to discomfort with parts of ourselves that seem messy, irrational, or vulnerable.

The Problem with Not Accepting Ourselves

When we're constantly trying to be someone we're not, several things happen:

- Wasted Energy: Mental and emotional energy is spent on

self-criticism and trying to force ourselves to fit in, instead of being channeled productively.

- Missed Connection: People are drawn to authenticity. Trying to present a curated version of ourselves hinders true connection.
- Diminished Creativity: Our best ideas come when we embrace our oddball tendencies. Self-rejection stifles this unique spark.
- Burnout and Resentment: The constant struggle to be perfect or to live up to others' expectations leads to exhaustion and a gnawing sense that we're not living our truth.

The Path to Wholeness: ENTP Self-Acceptance Strategies

1. Challenge the Negative Self-Talk: Those critical voices in our head? Don't believe their lies. Practice separating self-criticism from constructive feedback.
2. Celebrate the Quirks: The things that make you "weird" are what make you interesting. Own those interests, that offbeat humor, and conversational tangents that lead to unexpected brilliance.
3. Mindful Self-Compassion: Notice when you're beating yourself up. Treat yourself as you would a good friend who is struggling – with kindness and understanding.
4. Find Your People: Seek out friends, communities, or online spaces where your brand of enthusiastic nerdiness is embraced, not side-eyed.
5. The Humor Cure: The ability to laugh at ourselves, even lovingly mock our own absurdities, is incredibly powerful in disarming our inner critic.
6. Embrace Growth, Not Perfection: We're lifelong learners. Focus on progress, on becoming slightly better versions of ourselves, not on achieving an unattainable ideal.

The Gift of Radical Self-Acceptance

When ENTPs learn to truly accept themselves, something magical happens:

- Confidence That Doesn't Need Validation: We own our brilliance without needing constant external reassurance. This unshakeable confidence is magnetic.
- Deeper Relationships: When we're not putting on a facade, we allow others to know and love the true us, flaws and all.
- Unleashed Creativity: Our weird, winding thought processes thrive on self-acceptance. This leads to truly original ideas and solutions.
- Focus on What Matters: Instead of constantly expending energy on self-improvement, we channel it towards making an impact on the world.

Tips for Those Who Love an ENTP

- Celebrate the Oddball Brilliance: Focus on what makes them unique, not how they deviate from the norm.
- Encourage Authenticity: Create a space where they feel safe being their full, unfiltered selves, without fearing judgment.
- Be a Sounding Board: Listen to their quirky ideas without trying to "fix" them. Enthusiastic support fuels their spirit.
- Embrace the Chaos: Accept that life with an ENTP is unpredictable and wonderfully messy. If you want boring and predictable, you're with the wrong person.

ENTPs are messy, marvelous creatures. When we accept ourselves – our intellectual curiosity, our chaotic thought patterns, our occasional social awkwardness, and all the beautiful contradictions in between – we give ourselves the greatest gift of all: the freedom to simply be our wonderfully weird, exceptional, world-changing selves.

"WHAT IF?": THE QUESTION THAT FUELS US

Two words hold immense power for any ENTP: "What if?" They're the sparks that ignite our mental firestorms, launching us into explorations of possibilities, potential problems, and the hidden connections between everything.

The Benefits of Thinking in Possibilities

- Innovation Powerhouse: ENTPs see what is and imagine all that could be. This fuels our relentless drive to find better solutions, improve existing systems, and envision new ways of living and creating.
- Never a Dull Moment: The world is our playground, full of patterns to understand, puzzles to solve, and theories to debate. Boredom is seldom an issue when every situation sets our "what if" brains whirring.
- Spotting Potential: We see the promise in people or projects where others see limitations. This makes us great mentors, advocates, and champions of unconventional or overlooked ideas.
- Adaptability Kings & Queens: Our focus on possibilities makes us adaptable to change. We're more likely to see unexpected obstacles as opportunities for a new approach, rather than reasons to give up.

The "What If" Double-Edged Sword

Our infinite questioning can also create challenges:

- Analysis Paralysis: The sheer number of possibilities can overwhelm us, sometimes leading to inaction as we analyze endless scenarios.
- Dissatisfaction with the Current Reality: Constantly

envisioning how things could be better can make the present feel inadequate by comparison.

- Idea Overload: Our brains can overload trying to keep up with the torrent of "what ifs," leading to exhaustion and difficulty focusing on the task at hand.
- Appearing Scattered or Unreliable: We can jump excitedly from one possibility to the next, leaving others confused about our intentions or commitment.

Turning Our "What If" Powers Into Superpowers

1. Start with the Big Picture: Before diving into the endless possibilities, ask: "What is the ultimate goal or the core problem we're trying to solve?" This gives our "what ifs" direction.
2. Selective Deep Dives: It's impossible to thoroughly analyze every single "what if." Learn to sense which ones are truly worth the deep dive, and ruthlessly discard the rest.
3. From Possibility to Action: Capture those brilliant ideas, explore a few in-depth, but then pick one to bring to reality – even if it's a smaller-scale test to see if it has legs.
4. Collaboration as Key: Share your "what ifs" with others. Different perspectives can illuminate potential flaws, refine the possibilities, and spark even more innovative iterations.
5. Celebrate the Wins, Even Small Ones: Implementing a successful change, no matter how small, renews our motivation and combats the sense of unrealized potential.

Tips for Non-ENTPs:

- Don't Shut Down the "What Ifs": Even if they seem outlandish, hear the ENTP out. Those tangents might lead to valuable insights.
- Ask Clarifying Questions: "What if we try this?" can be vague. Encourage them to articulate specific potential solutions or improvements.
- Channel the Enthusiasm: Help the ENTP focus on one or two most promising "what ifs" to prevent them from scattering

energy too broadly.

- Appreciate the Long-Game: ENTPs are always thinking several steps ahead. Trust they have a bigger vision, even if the connecting path isn't immediately clear.

The World Needs the ENTP "What If" Mindset

We push boundaries, refuse to settle for "good enough," and imagine the seemingly impossible into existence. ENTPs challenge the status quo, not to cause senseless disruption, but because an unexamined status quo is an affront to all the potential waiting to be unleashed.

Our "what ifs" make us catalysts for change, sparks that ignite progress, and champions of creating a better, more interesting, more possibility-laden world. And yes, sometimes they drive ourselves and those around us a little bit mad in the process – but we believe it's a worthy trade-off.

EMBRACING THE JOURNEY: PERSONAL GROWTH FOR ENTPS

ENTPs are fascinated by growth in the external world – innovation, improvement, turning an idea into reality. However, when it comes to our own personal growth, things get a bit trickier. We can fall into the trap of always focusing outwards, neglecting the continuous inner work it takes to become the best possible version of ourselves.

Why Personal Growth Can Be Uncomfortable for ENTPs

1. Vulnerability Challenge: Growth means confronting our blind spots, those less-than-shiny parts we'd rather ignore. This vulnerability can cause major discomfort for ENTPs.
2. Fear of Losing Our Edge: We might worry that tackling emotional weaknesses or developing patience will blunt our intellectual edge or quick wit.
3. Perfectionism Trap: The idea of a never-ending journey rather than a clear end goal (perfect self? No thanks!) can feel discouraging before we even start.
4. Restlessness Gets in the Way: Slow, steady progress isn't our strong suit. We want rapid transformation, making it hard to stick with habits that yield gradual (but lasting) change.

Embracing Growth, the ENTP Way

Personal growth isn't about turning into someone we're not; it's about unlocking our full potential as thinkers, doers, and, yes, even feelers. Here's how to make it work for us:

- Reframe Growth as a Challenge: Instead of "fixing" ourselves, think of it as solving a complex puzzle. What areas hold untapped potential that, with some effort, could level up our abilities?

- Gamify the Process: Set small, achievable goals, track progress visually, and reward successes to keep motivation strong.
- Find the Growth Hook: Connect personal development to our passions. Want to be a better communicator? It'll make our arguments for world-changing ideas more persuasive.
- Focus on Strengths AND Weaknesses: Double down on what we're awesome at, while also dedicating some energy to shoring up blind spots that get in our way.
- Seek Non-Traditional Mentors: Look for guidance from those who excel in areas we struggle with, whether it's emotional intelligence, time management, or staying present in conversations.
- Make It an Experiment: Try a new habit for 30 days, track data on ourselves, analyze. This appeals to our scientific minds and reduces the emotional stakes.

Areas Where Growth Pays Off Big for ENTPs

- Emotional Intelligence: Improves our relationships, ability to influence others, and makes it easier to work collaboratively to bring our ideas to life.
- Communication Skills: Learning to convey our ideas clearly and persuasively, while truly listening to others, makes us an unstoppable force.
- Stress Management: Staying centered in the face of chaos and finding healthy stress outlets helps prevent burnout and keeps our creativity flowing.
- Follow-Through: Developing some discipline in seeing projects through to completion multiplies our impact on the world.

Tips for Supporting an ENTP's Growth:

- Acknowledge Their Efforts: Even small steps towards greater self-awareness or better habits deserve recognition.
- Focus on the Positives: Frame growth as unlocking additional awesomeness, rather than harping on

weaknesses.

-    Be Patient: Transformation for ENTPs rarely follows a linear path. Embrace their bursts of progress even if they're interspersed with periods of reverting to their old ways.
- Offer Accountability: Help them stay on track with their self-improvement goals, without turning into a nag.

Personal growth is a lifelong adventure, and for ENTPs that adventure will be full of excitement, unexpected detours, and major a-ha moments along the way. By recognizing growth as an essential part of our quest for knowledge, innovation, and making our mark on the world, we make ourselves better equipped to tackle any challenge with both our brilliant minds and compassionate, capable hearts.

THRIVING, NOT JUST SURVIVING: BUILDING A LIFE WE LOVE

ENTPs are full of potential. We have brilliant minds, boundless energy, and a burning desire to make an impact on the world. Yet, too often we end up feeling scattered, frustrated, or like we're falling short of that potential. Building a life that truly allows us to thrive – one that energizes us, feeds our passions, and aligns with our values – isn't automatic; it takes intention and a willingness to confront some uncomfortable truths.

Why ENTPs May Struggle to Thrive

- Too Many Options: Our love of possibilities can lead to decision fatigue or feeling paralyzed by the sheer number of potential paths we *could* take.
- Shiny Object Syndrome: We get excited about new ideas and projects but may lose interest when the initial spark fades, leaving a trail of half-started ventures.
- Conventional Success Doesn't Fit: Soul-sucking jobs with rigid routines, prioritizing status over meaning...this isn't a recipe for an ENTP to thrive, but it's an easy trap to fall into.
- Ignoring Our Need for Depth: We can get so swept up in the chase for novelty and stimulation that we neglect time for reflection, connection with our values, and truly processing internal experiences.

Finding Our "Thrive Zone"

Creating a fulfilling life as an ENTP requires answering a few crucial questions:

- What Sparks Our Excitement?: What are the activities, topics, or projects that leave us feeling energized, where we lose track of time and feel truly engaged?

- Where's Our Impact?: How do we want to make a difference in the world? What problems do we want to solve, or what kind of legacy do we want to leave behind?
- What Does Balance Look Like?: What mix of intellectual challenge, novelty, downtime, human connection, and creative expression do we need to feel our best?
- What Are We Willing to Sacrifice?: We can't have it all. Acknowledging the trade-offs we're willing to make helps us focus on what truly matters.

Building Blocks of a Thriving ENTP Life

1. Embrace "Good Enough": Done is better than perfect. We need to make peace with imperfection to free up time and energy to pursue the things that light us on fire.
2. Self-Imposed Structure: Just enough routine (flexible, and designed by us) creates room for our best work while minimizing overwhelm.
3. Seek Problems Worth Solving: Find challenges that tap into our strengths and match our desire to make a positive contribution.
4. Nurture Your People: ENTPs thrive with a supportive community who appreciate our quirks, challenge our ideas, and love us unconditionally.
5. Time for Reflection: Schedule time for introspection, journaling, or deep conversations to process experiences and make sure we're heading in the right direction.
6. Fuel the Engine: Our brains are high-performance machines. Healthy food, enough sleep, and movement are non-negotiable for optimal functioning and sustained energy.

Experiment and Iterate

Designing a thriving life is an ongoing experiment. Be prepared to make adjustments as you go:

- Try Before You Commit: "Test drive" potential major choices by volunteering, shadowing someone in the field, or taking trial courses.

- Reassess Regularly: What fueled us a year ago might not be a priority now. Regular check-ins with ourselves keep us aligned with our evolving desires.
- Celebrate the Quirky Path: There's no one-size-fits-all timeline for ENTPs. Embrace the zigs and zags as part of the journey.

Signs You're in Thrive Mode

- Boredom is (Mostly) Replaced by Engagement: Most of the time, you're excited by your projects, find your work meaningful, and see a path forward.
- Relationships Feel Nourishing: You have people who bring out your best, support your growth, and make you laugh until your sides hurt.
- A Sense of Flow: Time melts away when you're immersed in activities that align with your skills and passions.
- Energy AND Rest: You have both the drive to pursue your ambitions and also feel okay taking guilt-free downtime to recharge.

For Those Supporting an ENTP's Quest to Thrive:

- Don't Expect a Map: Our journey has twists and turns. Be a source of stability and encouragement while respecting our need to find our own way.
- Offer Practical Help: We suck at mundane tasks. Help with things like meal prep or scheduling frees up energy for our bigger pursuits.
- Listen Without Fixing: Sometimes we just need to vent or talk out loud to process. Resist the urge to jump in with solutions until asked.
- Celebrate the Victories: Acknowledge the effort, not just the outcome. This keeps our motivation strong during times of experimentation.

A thriving ENTP is a force of nature – a whirlwind of positive change, creative solutions, and unbridled enthusiasm. Building a life that allows us to flourish isn't always a straightforward path, but it's undoubtedly one that leaves the world a more vibrant, innovative, and possibility-rich place.

UNLEASH THE ENTP: A CALL TO ACTION

My dear fellow explorers, innovators, and relentless challengers of the ordinary, we've come to the exhilarating culmination of this journey. You've delved into the depths of your ENTP mind, laughed at its quirky brilliance, wrestled with its contradictions, and ultimately, embraced the magnificent power of your unique perspective. But understanding oneself is only half the battle. Now, it's time to take action!

Step 1: Embrace Your Disruptive Nature

The world is filled with well-trodden paths, rules carved in stone, and the stifling chorus of "that's how things have always been done." Your ENTP mind is a glorious wrecking ball designed to shatter this stagnant status quo. Don't fear being the voice that questions, the hand that raises in objection. Your ability to see flaws, poke holes in logic, and offer wildly creative alternatives is your superpower. Use it to disrupt outdated systems, ignite new ideas, and challenge the very foundations of how things 'should' be.

Step 2: Turn That Debate Brain Outward

Your inner world is a constant whirlwind of debates, arguments, and mental sparring matches. It's part of how you process, learn, and grow. But don't let all that brilliant discourse stay internal! Find your tribe - the people who won't just tolerate, but actively relish, your intellectual jousting. Seek out diverse perspectives, jump into fiery discussions, and revel in the delicious challenge of defending your ideas or having your mind spectacularly changed. This is your mental gym, where you'll sharpen your wit and broaden your understanding of the world.

Step 3: Fuel the Unquenchable Fire of Curiosity

Boredom is your kryptonite. Your mind craves novelty, complexity, and the thrill of the unexplored. Make a pact with yourself to never stop learning. Dive headfirst into subjects that intrigue you. Pick up a new hobby. Travel to places less traveled. Embrace the beginner's mindset with gusto, knowing that the joy lies in the pursuit rather than mastery. Your ENTP mind is an insatiable sponge; the world is your endlessly fascinating classroom.

Step 4: Build Your Bridge of Ideas

Your greatest strength is your ability to connect seemingly disparate dots, forging new pathways of thought where others see only chaos. But those brilliant leaps live in your head, and the world needs to witness them! Whether it's through writing, speaking, creating art, or spearheading innovative projects, find your medium of expression. Build bridges between your mental universe and the tangible world, sharing your unique vision and inspiring others to think bigger.

Step 5: Find Your Champions, and Champion Others

The ENTP journey can, at times, feel a bit lonely. Your quick wit and brutal honesty may not always win you popularity contests. But seek out those who value your authenticity, who are energized by your boundless enthusiasm, and who appreciate the way you make them see the world in a whole new light. Surround yourself with these champions, and in turn, champion others. Lift up those with potential, mentor those seeking direction, and celebrate the magnificent diversity of human thought with the open heart of a true ENTP.

The ENTP Charge

The world desperately needs your disruptive spirit, your relentless questioning, and your unbridled ability to imagine a better future. Don't settle for the confines of expectation.

Don't mute your intellectual spark. Step out with the audacious confidence that is your ENTP birthright and change the world in your own spectacular way.

Remember, this is not an ending, but the start of a grand adventure. Go forth, fellow ENTPs, and make some beautiful chaos.